Nineveh

ZOHAR ATKINS is a poet, rabbi and theologian, based in New York. He earned a DPhil in Theology from Balliol College, Oxford, where he was a Rhodes Scholar, and a BA and MA from Brown. He is the author of *An Ethical and Theological Appropriation of Heidegger's Critique of Modernity* (Palgrave Macmillan, 2018). His poetry won an Eric Gregory Award in 2018. Other poems have appeared in *New Poetries VII*, *Blackbox Manifold*, *The Glasgow Review of Books*, *PN Review*, *The Lehrhaus*, *TYPO*, and elsewhere. Atkins is the founder of *Etz Hasadeh*, a Center for Existential Torah Study, and a David Hartman Fellow at the *Shalom Hartman Institute of North America*.

ZOHAR ATKINS

Nineveh

CARCANET

First published in Great Britain in 2019 by
Carcanet Press Ltd
Alliance House, 30 Cross Street
Manchester M2 7AQ
www.carcanet.co.uk

Text copyright © Zohar Atkins, 2019

A CIP catalogue record for this book is available from the British Library.
ISBN 978 1 784107 39 0

The publisher acknowledges financial assistance from Arts Council England.

Typeset in England by XL Publishing Services, Exmouth
Printed and bound in England by SRP Ltd, Exeter

Contents

Nineveh

Protest

No sooner do I say
'Let there be light'
Then a horde of angels arrives
With their signs.

'No more oppression of darkness!'
'Stop occupying our empty wild.'
'Down with the visible!'
'God Should Know Better Than to Speak.'

Even the walls of my hotel lobby seem
To sing out against me.
But then I remember, I'm God.
Soon the angels will want to go home.

In the end, nobody will remember how they
Held hands, soaring together, like a school
Into the tear-dusk firmament.
How they laid their celestial torsos down in a row

To prove my world a desecration.
Nobody will hear their words of lament,
'Holy, holy, holy', as anything
But praise.

System Baby

I was six when I first filed for moral bankruptcy.
I was ten when they told me language is inherently *classist*.
At thirteen, I started defining kindness
as 'making nice to those who like your favorite teams'.
At twenty, I hired a ghost to write my LinkedIn profile.
At thirty, I started radiosuctive parole therapy.
At forty-one, I began to look sideways and call it *inward*.
At eighty-six, I'm a work in progress.
Today, at 120, I'm a proud piece of gum,
who's almost forgotten the countless nights it took me,
locked in the shoe of the human mind,
to get here to tell you: don't let others humanise you.
Don't let them take away your objectivity
no matter how much they brutalise you.

The Sin

According to the *Zohar*, a sin is never as defiant as it seems.
Rather, the sin, if it can be so called, always comes
from too much of what is proper.

The builders' sin, for example, was not
that they breached the heavenly palace,
but that they stopped at the first gate.

Others say the sin was that they made the tower resemble a deity.
The builders had placed a sword in the tower's hand
like children drawing on the cover of *Time*.

Others say the sin was that they had taken a natural word, 'Babel'
and leveraged it into the brand of a Multinational Consulting Group.
This is the true meaning of 'Let us make a name for ourselves'.

No one agrees.
As if the scattering of tongues in the story were a cipher
for the interpretive chaos to come.

To this day, we continue to debate what bricks to use.
Should they be made of rice paper or holograph?
Should the tower's shadow be cut through enemy airspace?
Can folks in PR really be called *builders*?

I still can't find the word *sin* anywhere in the story.

Fake Judaism

Abraham, says Deleuze,
could only become a Jew
by first being a *goy*.

Inside every *pintele yid*
is a Pinteresting Gentile.
And inside every Gentile

is a unique ignorance
of the Midrash
that the Torah was given to everyone.

★

I have studied the yud-shaped pool of blood
like an exhausted hunter sniffing out the air for some lentils.

I have adorned myself with Bilaam's staff infection, and the lines on
    my face
record the litany of psalms I have struggled
to compose
lisping, tongue-numb from the frost of imagined taiga.

But never could I hear
the night-ram bleating out
Zohar, Zohar.

★

I've heard Bialik forbade himself from writing as a kind of sign-
    prophecy.
A desperate gesture towards the emptiness of his devotional
    rebellion.

The way Hosea names his daughter 'Ee-Ruchama', meaning there
   is no mercy,
to demonstrate that God, too, will have no mercy on his children.

The poet's silence is an almond-shaped abandonment.

Holiness, an incorrect password
to a door that has no lock, no gatekeeper.

★

To be a Jew is to pervert metaphysics
so that what matters is not ideas
about the thing or the thing itself

but the voice, departing into blessing.
A piece of fruit, embezzled from paradise
by speech alone. By speech, alone.

The Binding of Isaac

Twenty minutes away, a young Muslim is dying of bone cancer
In an Israeli hospital. His sister refuses to donate her marrow
And the young man cries out in darkness, 'Allah, Merciful One,
   I know
You are punishing me for all those naked women I visited'.
And under his rage is the sadness of tank-ploughed olive groves.
We read about it in our seminar and debate the pros and cons
Of hugging him. We refer to human touch as an intervention.
'Who are you to love me?' We hear our fantasies shout back at us.
And so it was that Abraham, having heard the angel's voice
And felt her tears, untied his only son, saying, 'God has provided
The offering for us'. But Ishmael insisted Avraham had heard wrong
And said, 'My place is here, on the altar'. And Abraham said,
   'Isaac, Isaac'.
And Ishmael said, '*Hineini*'.

Some Pogs

After John Ashbery

These are amassing: each
Striking a neighbor, as though speech
Were a rote performance.
Arranging by class

To meet as far as this passage
From the world as collecting
With it, you and I
Are suddenly what the pogs try

To tell us we are:
That there, merely being there
Means something; that soon
We may thrash, horde, replay.

And glad not to have invented
Such nerdiness, we are surrounded:
A silence filled with noises,
A score-board on which emerges

A chorus of grunts, a boyish morning.
Flipped in a halogen light, and moving,
Our memories put on such brilliance
These accents seam their own events.

Fugue or Fondue?

I

For what duration
can purpose be
suspended?

A question like vinegar
and mustard, like
an unmowed lawn.

Answers like beloveds seem
not the one. Like you assumes
unnamed berries poisonous.

II

'Knowledge needs ignorance
as vision needs shade',
says Ockham,

the apocryphal lilacs,
cavities, fledgling
similitude.

Fugue or fondue?
Directions take time
to dissolve.

III

But, what of the sea,
the hidden boat one
with the threatening wave?

What of distance
shores faint
against the lurking eye?

What of your fear,
the unsubstantiated word
substantiated?

Outside Echoes

The best way to satisfy your baby
    is surely
    not by junking it.

Start again with smoke
    on the face
    of distinction.

Start with the neutral-
    ised myth of
    necessary ancestors.

I knew it was a lie
    to use signs
    you would take

As colonial, but *nu*?
    We were playing
    it out, each

Turn a negation
    split to accord
    what no time can

Afford. Let the page
    dictate you
    for a change.

Let meno-pause
    be literal, hot
    as an archetype.

Let the typography
    of state violence
    not be charmed

Through proximity.
   Notice the Guatemalan
   figure placing onions

And peppers
   back in their proper
   stall.

Will you prefer the hedge
   fund manager
   with the blind daughter

Over the night-shift golem?
   Will you point out
   the false logic

Of this binary
   and not see that you also
   use it? Today's thieves

Are tomorrow's resisters.
   Today's desecrators
   are yesterday's

Sanctifiers. So,
   your anthropologist friend
   waxes syntax

Avoidance as the new
   'farting silently'.
   A still small voice

Is smelt. Whoever
   dealt us tradition
   dealt us our hands.

None of this stops
      occupation or hypocrisy,
      the prophet's excrescence

From the foam of nihilism.
      None of it brings back
      the Baghdadi mule-driver

Who knew himself to be the whole
      as he penetrated his trusted
      friend, the one he had named

Ohad. We stand at
      a gas station, waiting
      for a transport to spirit

Possession. Or
      we stand at the peak
      of knowing

Good and evil:
      pacemakers produced
      by Congolese children.

What's mine
      is mined. What's yours
      is mined.

And the mind is quality
      as sky. Is money.
      Is the difference

Between yes and no
      I and why,
      fall and fly.

Offer it:
        Offer your failure
        to contain yourself.

Offer the strings
        which hold you
        down

And the scissors
        which cause you
        to arise

Like an army of angels
        in search of their general,
        a story that can direct

Them back
        towards identity,
        cast their movement

Into mission, color into
        shape, urge into
        freedom.

'You've been reading too
        much Hegel',
        she says,

And I say,
        'The line between speculation
        and truth is like the line

Between creature and Creator'.
        We had been drinking
        coffee, and eating

Lox – she abstained
        from the Lox,
        but joined me

In the act of having them
        as referents
        on our table.

You want me
        to treat your grandmother
        to her fantasies,

But what about the man
        holding up the sign, saying,
        'Jews Control Everything

Google It'? What
        about the masturbator
        whose only wish is to be

Witnessed
        for who he is,
        a sex magician?

Can we have fairy-tales
        without monsters?
        Can we have feminism

Without the added trauma
        of failing to have
        it all?

'Reason without spirit
        is bureaucracy.
        Spirit without

Reason is absurdity',
		says the philosopher
		pretending to be a rhetorician.

'We need more dogs
		in leopard-skin dresses
		in strollers',

Jests the winter
		in and around us.
		More life surpassing questions.

Déjà Vu

Tell me the absence of helicopters, there
In winter blue, above the bridge, isn't

Significant – that the upside-down sign
Advertising a world at No Additional Fees

Isn't meant to draw us into it.
And poems, tell me the years don't spread,

Vainly forming a notion
Of self-worth and haggling over the boundary

Between voice and desire. Tell me this need
To hibernate is language's way of teasing

Forth from refusal. Tell me this staff, this rock
This comma, projected into bread and blessing

Doesn't tell us everything we need to know to morph
To ward to throw unknowable music: Fire, child of snow

And snow, child of gaze. Whose? Yes. That's the point,
O chaos. So may the target of our senses and the backlog

Of our failures be constitutive of our lives that we may live
Beyond allure. Let those orange suede boots traipsing across

Your poem not dissolve your knowledge that you manifested
From a rat's periphery. She wants to be a co-author with you,

As if you were the same as you. As if the you deciding which
Words deserve to arrive – here – were not an effect of the words

They only seem to chaperone. Tell me a truth that doesn't
Reference Heidegger, a love whose knowledge exceeds all scope.

Seeker's Psalm

And Dinah, daughter of Leah,
little girl of Jacob, went out to look
upon the daughters of the land.

(Gen. 34:1)

Our God and God of our ancestors,
have we not also gone out to find ourselves
amongst the peoples of the world?

Have we not also left our parents' homes
in search of old questions and new light?

What was Dinah seeking when she was seen
by Shechem ben Hamor?

What image of you formed in her eyes
before she was taken by him –
taken first by force and then by love?

God who lifts mountains
over us
so we may accept your shadow

God who mines order from chaos
music from noise
struggle from conformity

God who leads us
astray
to a place we will show you

Keep us as you kept Dinah –
in the palace of Shechem

so even here
far from our origins
we may stay

Yisrael

Descent

And Joseph saw his brothers, and knew them
And made himself strange to them
And spoke roughly to them.

(Genesis 42:7)

He made himself strange to them.
We might think this means he hid himself

But commentaries, rescued by chance
From the offal of Fallujah, and sold

On the black market to collectors
From Hebrew U, tell otherwise.

At Tel Aviv, they say this is a fiction,
That the site of rescue was Leipzig, 1939.

There are wonders not even the human heart can save.
Can you imagine the entire Talmud

Burnt forever? Can you imagine not having heard
Of anything you assume makes a world?

Tree, stone, earth? 'It was his very strangeness
That he hoped would out him', says Rashbam.

As if Joseph still needs us to see he's truly Joseph,
And not Pharaoh's double,

The guy Pharaoh will forget.
Joseph remembers who he is.

He is the only character in the Bible who weeps seven times,
Once for each day of Creation.

We thought we'd traded Joseph in for a life free of disturbance.
Now he sells us corn, but won't take our money.

Meanwhile, the socialists picket, 'Where is Zebulon's chapter and
    Naftali's
And Issasschar's and Gad's?' If only Benjamin could have lived a
    year longer

Just to have written an essay redeeming the hanged baker.
We might have read theories suggesting

Dream interpretation was then what consulting is now.
Joseph was just looking at the numbers.

Song of Myself (Apocryphal)

I am my own listserve,
advertising job and fellowship opportunities
for myself by myself to myself.

I sing of unpaid internships to my soul, O soul,
and of passing controversies on which to take sides
is to take the side of the self.

I re-post myself and forward myself
and respond to myself with emojis
for I am the screen and its anticipation,

the pleasure of being liked
and of commanding myself to like others.
For all pages are contained in my potential

for sharing, scrolling, even viewing
incognito. I sign in on myself
and log out of myself and yet remain

more than my usernames
and forgotten passwords.
For I am the great web itself

and every parody known to it
is known to me, and every troll
who devastates its comments section

is of myself. I am celebrity culture
and conspiracy theory culture –
the metastasis of meaning

that nurtures both political
gossip and culture wars,
food blogs, parenting blogs,

and cat videos. What you
shall click, I shall click,
and where you shall cut and paste

I shall be cut and paste.
Do I make myself redundant?
Very well then, I make myself

redundant. I am a paywall
(disambiguation)
I contain metadata.

The Oy of the Poyem: 28 Exercises in non-Mastery

Click here for 29 reasons
you are not *not* Mark Ruffalo.

Click here for 6 proofs
Buzzfeed is a distraction from the Buzzfeed as such.

Click Next to receive yourself as a coupon.
Click Play Now to become forever.

Click Incognito Mode to avoid the paywall,
discover 10 myths you thought were facts.

If the font ain't Calypso, switch to Reality.
If Reality ain't high definition,

petition your senator here.
Each day, thousands of innocents

lack yoghurt, political will,
and courage to wear bright clothing.

Coincidence? Each second
you give to thinking

will be matched by thirty minutes
of callousness, regret, and avoidance.

Click here to short your cynicism,
make millions in emerging emotional markets.

In the long-run, even mavericks fall
on one side of the fence, wondering

why they didn't learn Esperanto.
In the short-run we are all unborn.

'That wasn't 28.'
'Nu? So it wasn't 28.'

Poetry TedTalk Notes

Most poetry has the same shelf life as the technology of its time.
Therefore, poetry is less about the individual poem, than about
the brand, the update, the plan, the package, the network, the
merger, the deal.
The question isn't 'Is this a good poem?' but, 'Is it scaleable?'
A poem, like a business, should always have an exit strategy.
A poem is a platform.
You can't solve all of poetry's problems in one poem, but you can
use it to build your profile, make connections, plant seeds.
The poverty of poetry is an asset.
The meaning of poetry isn't liquid.
Carried interest in poetry is essentially tax-free.
Reading is a better return on investment than writing.

Poetry Is Failure by Other Means

Rift becomes drift.
Drift becomes draft,
and riven,
we drive on.

A rift is a raft, rife with drivel
and rivaling our aptitude
for rapture.
Daft is the new deft.

Defy trying, deify vying.
Faff.
So we roved,
draughts over the farthest ear,

here, where there is nothing
feared that is not heard. And nothing
heard that is not weird
or nothing weird that is not fed further off.

Soundbytes

We exist by virtue of God's masochism,
a self-inflicted otherness,
a sailing shipwreck,
tweeted the pope.

That is why we must meditate
on marble as if it were flesh,
cajole ourselves for wanting
one final cannoli

or be nonplussed.
It is why words are vultures,
and myth will forever be myth,
according to the latest numbers.

It is why genius is destiny,
and I could have been anywhere
and anyone,
but I am here and me.

Or how your hand cream augurs
augury itself
as hand cream,
flashing truth as an emoticon.

Tosefta

Rav Kahana told the story that

Rav Hisda said

    In all my days, I was considered a master of planting and
        collecting,
    yet when I went out to trim the vineyards,
    I cut too close to the vine.
    Now, people will say, it would be better if I hadn't trimmed at all.

To which Abaye said

    The branches shall return,
    the leaves shall return,
    and the fruit shall return.
    The only thing you have shorn is yourself.

    Said Rav Hisda
    But what harvest can there be in the meantime?

    Said Abaye
    If one goes out as a harvester, one shall return a harvester.

Rav Nachman bar Yitzchak gave a different account.

    He said Rav Hisda was concerned about an imperfection
    around his genitals
    he had revealed while grooming himself.

Rav Hisda said

    The shears that should have been my exaltation
    have become my demise.
    What will my wife say when she sees me like this?

Abaye sought to console him

First, your imperfection will soon be covered,
second, it is not an imperfection,
and third, if it is an imperfection, your wife will not see it as such.

Rav Pappa recounted it differently.

Rav Hisda was depressed
because all the days of his life he had been meticulous in his
prayers,
yet when it came time for him to lead *Hallel* on *Rosh Chodesh*
he forgot all of the words, except for the opening blessing.

He said to himself
On what will my blessing carry?

Abaye said
On your silence.

Rav Hisda objected that one cannot praise in silence.

Abaye said
First, your silence shall soon turn to song,
second, it already is a kind of song,
and third, even if you never sing again,
your students shall respond "Amen" all the same.

Rav Hisda retorted
I am not worried about my students,
but about the One Who Speaks and Worlds Come To Presence.

Said Abaye
If one approaches with the hope that he will listen,
he will listen.

Say

After Peter Gizzi after Wallace Stevens

Say life is the jetlag of angels
flying red-eye from redemption
to the now.

Say every measured thing is a pixel
of some divine heartbreak.

Say that Sabbath is a hammer.
Is a hammer?
That Sabbath comes too soon.

Say the empty hands of strangers
carry their own potential –
for stabbing. Or typing.

Say each world's decided
in the rift where seeking fails,
in the distorted light of psalm-

catastrophe. Say again, say better.
Say that the wrath of the hermit
And the fright of the gatekeeper

are one, must be one. Are alluded
to in the projected Scripture
grasped and missed by tradition.

Say the animals, too, are preparing, frantically,
to greet their Sabbath Queen,
that the bark and squawk of mingled beings

thumping over the last sighs of traffic
compose a poem no author could write
without being changed.

Say the created world is nothing but a promise
of commentary, that soon, everything will be
recorded in the *Book of Next Time.*

Say this form is borrowed and you know
the reference. Do you really know it?
Say *say.* Googletranslate the inarticulate,

the hoarded wonder lodged forgotten
in your side. Where is your body
in all of this? Where is the body

in relation to the concept of 'you'?
Say 'I' and 'you' are nicknames
given to us by the Magnificent.

Is it cheating to break rules that don't exist?
And what will you do for the refugees
that pour through the borders of Mind?

But come, my Beloved.
It is nearly time for the perceived world
to be accompanied by what is missing from it.

Say *peace.* Say *bless.* Say nothing.

Dear Guru

Dear Guru,
source of ideation and aesthetically tested angst,
maker of all things your consumers pronounce
enlightened,
you who are beyond subject
and, let's not kid ourselves, object,
you who are the whoopy cushion of all metaphors,
and for whom it is a sin even to say you are,
forgive me for calling on you for such a small favor,
I know you are very busy, holding on the line
with Verizon customer service. But
I do not know how to write poetry, guru.
Teach me your ways that my words
may one day ally themselves with words
that are not mine, so the language will not mock me
or bamboozle me or take me for a ride or what
have you, so I will not be the butt of language's
cigarette anthropologists stomp on during their
lunch break. Dear guru, rescue me from the belly
of truth, in whose mouth I threw myself to hide
from you. Send me back to the Nineveh of ordinary
language, where sandwich wrappers are just
sandwich wrappers and eulogies consist entirely
of emojis. Guru, give me the wisdom you told me
I already have, if only I would lose five pounds,
or my obsession with losing weight, or my thought
or my hunger for knowledge and metaphor
and footnotes. The wisdom to stop calling
on you at such late hours. Or the wisdom to
stop calling you by your title or your middle name
(Kony? Ted? Usurpulus?) and start calling
you by your last name, which is guru
spelled backwards: urug, if only
I could pronounce it.

Dementia

Jacob wakes and sees the woman of his dreams is not the person lying next to him, massaging his neck. Can he love her anyways? Can he love Rachel by loving Leah? He reaches for the nearest commentary, seeking comfort: 'The voice was the voice of Rachel, but the body was the body of Leah.'

It's not Rachel's fault she's demented. But without a conniving Lavan or a wily Rebecca, who can Jacob blame but himself? The love is there, but it's almost like the love of an old man for his heirloom watch. And what does Leah know? She is like a Rachel who wants Jacob to know she's Rachel, but is stuck in the body of Leah. Whenever Jacob asks her 'How are you?' Leah says, 'Fine', but under the bed of Leah's body, Rachel is crying out for Jacob to look harder.

Letting Nothing Wait

Numb to the fascism of ordinary things
the reported chaos of listicles

the ambient panic of winter sky
pretending everything is fine

your hands perform their necessary
crunching while your mind runs

critical calculations. I talk to myself
about writing a poem

and the uselessness of being
clear in an age of segregated tears.

I am already aware this poem,
like perhaps every poem right now,

has
become bad –

too much tell, too political,
not enough misdirection

or else, not enough tell, too apolitical,
too much direction.

The language is coarse
like celebrity hair implants

and the private misery of fish.
Coarse and hungry, like a full belly

is full of regret
and a sharper apprehension of cosmic emptiness.

I am already aware of what a pushover I am
to be writing poems while people are out

clamoring in the televised streets
and perhaps you will love me

since you, if you are reading this,
are also likely a pushover.

Perhaps this covenant between us will serve to reinforce
our feelings of moral safety, which, we hope, are our best chance of
   payback

for a lifetime of getting kicked around by meanie-butts,
who drown out our cries with History's laugh track and claim it's live.

Villanelle

Every villanelle man writes inclines towards vanity.
For God's help is no help to measure line by line.
And every thought man hypes elides insanity.

Like the rhetorician's speech, whose rose becomes profanity,
a peeling trophy of the shelled-out mind.
Every villanelle man writes inclines towards vanity.

And who can spare the poor imagination its reality?
Unveil the self-consuming subject as a sign?
For every thought man hypes elides insanity.

'Only nothing is', the mystic player howls, portending actuality,
knowing, as he speaks, the contradiction of his wisdom, too
    perennial for time.
Every villanelle man writes inclines towards vanity.

Yet Abraham – we read – discovered God in hospitality,
And at the borders of his tent refused to utter 'mine'.
But caution: Every thought man hypes elides insanity.

Might each relic make the world a jar for its humanity?
Each body needing soul its life divine?
Every villanelle man writes inclines towards vanity.
And every thought man hypes elides insanity.

Hermeneutics

I ask the giant
If he wants my seat.

Either he doesn't hear me
Or he doesn't want to.

What Did the Heavenly Ministers Do?

What did the heavenly ministers do
when they found God eating
on a fast day?

One said, 'We don't rule from the Holy
One, May His Name Be Blessed'.
One said, 'There is no day

and night in Heaven'.
One said, 'The Lord needs us to teach him
in the ways of his World'.

One said, 'God eats, but he makes his food taste like ash'.
And One said, 'For God, fasting has no meaning,
since the Lord has no appetite'.

From this it can be derived
that to fulfill the *mitzvah* of fasting,
God watches *Schindler's List* instead.

'What did God do before the Holocaust?'
One angel asked.
Another asked, 'What did God do before film?'

They answered in unison: 'There is no before
and after in the Torah.'

In the Beginning

Before God could separate the upper and the lower worlds, light from day, earth from water, he was sitting in a tiny room, unable to move. Whenever his mouth would begin to open to say, 'Let there be', he would be overcome. Each day, God would wake up, intending to create the world, and each day, God would be unable. Sometimes he'd find a physical reason. His hands were too shaky. Other times, he'd find a distraction. God surrounded himself with blueprints of his world, but the execution was not something he could bring himself to do. Perhaps, on some level, God understood that the Creation of the World was also his goodbye, the inauguration of a world that would grow not to need him. Was he ready to write himself out of existence just yet? So Gabriel came before the Lord and said, 'I know you are afraid. I know the world you'll make will not be perfect, that it will only be one possible world and not the ideal world in your mind. But if you impart to it all of your love, you will find peace.'

Cain and Abel

Cain was the first to present his power point on inspirational
    leadership.
His argument was tight and his slides were sleek.
Everything supported his core message: No poetry without
    readership.
When he finished, he looked out. The great hall was empty.

Abel went second. The room filled and there were hors d'oervres a
    plenty.
He spoke without notes and in praise of prose. His voice was meek.
No one could hear a thing, but what they could
Convinced them to appoint him sentry.

Cain was standing in the back. His face fell. His bowtie crumbled
    into paint.
A fire alarm went off, as if the universe could hear his sole complaint.
'Why is your face fallen? Haven't you heard of re-entry?'
How could he respond to such a question when he was feeling so
    bleak?

And besides, why was a fire alarm talking to him?
'If you hire a new head of sales, all is well', it said,
'But if not, bankruptcy poses in baby cobra at the New York office.'
Cain was perplexed. This was like nothing he had ever read.

So Cain turned to congratulate Abel.
He considered using the nearest mic to bash in his head.
But thanks to his leadership coach, he took some breaths
And recentered instead.

Abel told Cain about his new prose initiative,
Invited him to join, assuming he was able.
Cain said, 'Can I get back to you by Friday?'
Abel said, 'I need to know now'.

So Cain said, 'No'.
It was no small thing for him to take a vow.
Who was this guy to be so pushy, anyhow?
At that moment, 'Young Abel collapsed'.

The cause of death, the doctors said, was inconclusive.
Some say drugs, others shame.
Some say every explanation's a fable –
We can neither blame Cain nor Abel.

Radish

How can I begin my tale
when I am still in it?

I pulled a radish from the ground
and found the ground more deep
than what my eyes had opened.

Beneath the spot,
another sapling formed
so that the vanity of my urgency
grew in measure with my obstinacy.

Soon, I was surrounded by radishes
so enormous I regretted being born.
I stopped to write this poem,
hoping it would help. But, even here,
before I end, is another radish.

Teraphim

Our precise meaning unknown
(say the dictionaries)
we rest in the shade of the familiar.

Some call us household gods,
others simply hide us under

the body's floorboards
or leave us out, forged,
on the mantel over the Mind.

I am used to serving as a decoy
for things more powerful than myself:

kings and witches and poverty.
I am the wanted and the unwanted.

Illicit, yet banal, harmless.
Like an over-the-counter drug.
Commonly accepted, yet taboo.

Scholars say I am powerless, except
when accompanied by incantation,
astral know-how, ornaments and cloaks.

It's true that, alone, I am nothing.
But I am easily activated, even by the smallest,
most apprenticed touch.

Whoever touches me will, indeed, know
the future.

Know the future as intimately as a household god
knows its place
will soon be erased

just as it has erased others
leaving only the shape
of a mouth that clings to my name, because it has nothing else.

Prayer

Dear Lord
Let me delete Uber

Without gloating about it
On social media

Let it be one of our many secrets
Like the time you caught me

Wishing I knew Yiddish
As I watched your two servants

Touch each other in the bathhouse
Or the time I saw the tops of houses

Poking through an open field
And thought it was the set

Of a film by Tarkovsky, or Eisenstein
Because I couldn't fathom that a people had lived

There.
Forgive me

For not saying
'Who made miracles in this place'

When I read Bialik or pass
Over a tree where you hung

Three innocents instead of five
And forgive me

For letting my imagination swallow me
Like Korach

Mistakenly swallowed chewing tobacco
And Moses swallowed his words

And Aaron swallowed his silence
And Miriam swallowed her song

Let me enter your plexiglass
Covered cathedral

Swim through your cellophane ears
And return not to tell the tale

But to become it
Lord, ripen my neurosis

Let each sinful thought keeping me
From you

Find its place
Kneaded in your montage

Rahab

Scholars imagine my body as a kind of manna.
My reception history is pregnant with evidence
supporting the idea
that the meaning of my flesh
and the flesh of my meaning are one,
that I embody a perfect correspondence
of world and fantasy,
am as capacious as my name says I am.
My devotees know me as a sea-goddess.
My critics identify me by my occupation – 'whore'.
They're not wrong.
I've been turning tricks since I was ten.
The point of my story is not what I have done
but what I have undone.
I'm the only virgin who became so
by sleeping with whoever asked.
Like the Jews, I, too, spent forty years
cruising for false gods in the wilderness.
And like the Jews, my turn to faith also came
through disappointment.
Monotheism is not about belief
but reticence.

Where, Oh Lord?

After Yehuda HaLevi

Where, Oh Lord,
can I find you?
Your place is rural and unsurveilled.

And where, Oh Lord,
can I miss you?
The whole world is your holiday home.

The angels retweet your thunder
yet your silence needs no introduction.

You are right here, on the Queensborough Bridge,
yet your fat ass makes the spheres seem like skinny jeans.

You are closer to things than their own thingliness,
yet reveal yourself only to skeptics, as their vanishing point.

I look for you and find you looking for me.
I ask for your number and you ask for mine.

But life must go on.
Papers must be written about immanence and transcendence.

Can such earthbound idiocy really be your dwelling place?
What temple, fashioned from your own clay, could possibly
   accommodate you?

You are exalted on nature's voiceless palanquin;
your throne is gentrified by human prayer.

And yet you are their author, editor, agent,
chief marketing officer, and head of sales.

Each moment is your *ars poetica*.

Lord, You Know

Lord, you know
the redundant exercises of my heart;
you alone can read the sonogram
of my foolish verse.

I remove my earplugs
and still you are there
in the false fire alarm
damaging my senses.

When Doeg the Edomite
appears in our seminar
I can always count on you
to rectify my misplaced accent.

Lord, you know
the redundant exercises of my heart;
you alone can read the sonogram
of my foolish verse.

Praying with My Feet

Foot after clobbered foot
I pantomime my Master's lisp
hoping

this formalism
will live up
to what I know

my careful copying
can only desecrate.

And if it does not?
If it only hangs by
a hashtag

takes a wrong exit
and finds the world
in inverted commas?

Gets eternally distracted
by renunciations
of Eden?

If, praying,
I wind up
on the cover of an abyss

and am praised
for pleasing
my stakeholders in nonbeing

I will be no further
than where I am
now,

revising myself
to look less
like Moses

and more
like Zohar
or less like a comparison

and more like Mike
revising my revisions
so that idolatry appears

to be the belief
that a poem can be finished
and the great illusion

which the good Lord demands
as recompense
for his eternal need

to terminate Creation
and switch careers;
maybe this time something

more purpose oriented
and less responsive
to public opinion.

CV

Before arriving here
I did a brief four-year residency
at Dachau where I focused
on the anthropology of marginalised groups.
My subject position was amenable
to the field work necessary for my research.
My methodology was 'deep embeddedness'
in the cultural forms of Nazi performativity
and vernacular choreography.
Attending to the semiotic *aporiae*
of ideology, I was able to deconstruct
the distinction between guard
and guarded, camp world and the world
as theoretical object, while simultaneous-
ly maintaing it. I am most resentful
however, of the unpaid emotional labor
I invested in counseling fellow victims
and negotiating my own survivor's guilt.
And there were times when being called
a *Musselman* felt like a microagression.
I was gaslighted so much I nearly
convinced myself I *was* dead.
Or worse, a man who had purchased
his life by agreeing to be permanently
detached from it.

Self-Portrait As a Poetry Bot

Alumnae of the Void,
we measure our loyalty
in clicks and non-fungible
donations.

We measure our loyalty
against our guilt of never
being enough,
never opening email.

Against our guilt of never
showing up, or as we say
in today's culture,
making ourselves visible.

Showing up, or as we say
Leaving Egypt,
meaning a world
without fanfare.

Leaving Egypt,
we are like stars
leaving daylight
to become markers of night.

We are like stars
whose arrival designates
the time of comparison
between priests and beggars.

Whose arrival is called 'Creation'
and requires a red carpet
of interpretation
or no carpet at all.

And requires a red carpet
of wonder
at how such terms formed
an encyclopedia of misdirection.

Of wonder
we are but a satellite,
an off-shore account
waiting to be dissolved.

We are but a satellite
and yet are we not also a center
whose periphery is wonder?
Waiting to be dissolved

an encyclopedia of misdirection
or no carpet at all
between priests and beggars
to become markers of night

without fanfare
making ourselves visible
never opening email
who can say

we are not loyal alumnae
clicking, donating our being
to some Void
some Egypt of guilt and wonder.

Apologies in Advance

I'm sorry for drawing your attention
to this
but better sooner than now.

Now that I'm no longer
sounding logical
you must decide

is it me or you,
madness, defiance, brilliance
over our heads

laziness or something
else, and how do you feel
about having a bio

you trust
thrust you with inspirational quotes
from a virulent antisemite (and I mean *virulent*)?

You see how quickly it devolves?
But it's not your stuff.
I'll name it. It's the fact that

language makes it unsafe
for you to interpret language.
It's the fact that you can't tell if misunderstanding

is a joke on which you are in
or of which you are the butt
and which, regardless, upsets you

because you are a stay-at-home politician
with more debt than it pays
to be alienated from

the junkmail continues
to mispell your name.
Not only that

you haven't prayed
since you discovered
you grew up

in a home that was spiritual
but not *spirituelle*.
And damn it, this poem

wasn't even intended
for you, but there's no way
to unsubscribe

unless you hit reply all
which is what you are doing
if you are reading this, like it or nah.

Innocence Is Never Luxuriant

Innocence is never luxuriant
is the kind of thing you must learn
through repetition

If you are the kind of thing
who seeks abstract wisdom
why not celebrate it

And if you are not
you must luxuriate in your innocence
which is already lost

By the time you have read this far
you will mistake wisdom
for repetition

It is imperative
never to let your innocence
get to your head

To get ahead
try withstanding imperatives
without repeating yourself

Or seeming alternative
is easy for you to say
but hard for you to hear

Knowing all things
will be archived
and therefore belonging

To a future
whose non-arrival
makes now possible

If you are the kind of thing
who's into that kind of thing
and you are

Why not make it better
less conditional
and more what it is

Innocent as luxury
luxurious as as
wise as repetition is abstract

Requires you to rewrite
your life, a future
whose non-arrival

Makes now possible

Subway Poem

No longer an avatar of myself
I copy a broken link,
saving image as a driven leaf
is recommended
in a shopping cart I cannot see
whose rewards are so many points
I can exchange for trips and tips
to log my visits, as if leaving
were an omen
priority class is proof
of providence accumulating
and ritual theory were not
it's own form of ritual,
the kind where Abraham realises
he's in a blockbuster movie
and decides to donate the proceeds
to cure the eye disease
uniquely caused
by watching

These Gyros of Inattention

These gyros of inattention and dross
These dopamine castles and ziggurats of sass
These rhetorical spools corrected to spoils
in a manuscript above our price range
these idolizations of God these exploitations of Man
and Woman these utopian translations
coerced by invisible, solitary wisdom mongers these hungers
become their own sapphire of affluence their own Edenic forgery
their own inflected factory of forms of ontological idiocy
their own palace of insanity their own den of rivalry
their own hoax at sorcery their own emblazoned prophecy
although I the Lord your God am Lord
of drones and honesty. Am holy as only the Lord can be
and say unto you be holy, as far as the mind can flee.

Sent

After Genesis 34

daughter of
daughters of land

son of
prince of land

saw took lay
humbled

cleaved daughter
loved
spoke

damsel damsel
spoke to father
damsel to wife

heard defiled daughter
sons were with cattle
in field
held peace came

father went out
to speak

sons came from field
heard grieved angered
done what shouldn't be done

spoke longs pray
give wife
make marriages
give daughters take daughters

dwell land dwell trade
take possession

said find favor
say give

ask give say
damsel to wife
answered spoke defiled sister

said cannot give uncircumcised
consent be circumcised

give daughters take daughters dwell
become one people

hearken circumcised take daughter
gone

pleased son
young man deferred
delight daughter
honored father

son came to gate of city
spoke men

dwell land trade
behold: land is large
take daughters for wives give daughters

consent to dwell
become one people
circumcised circumcised

cattle and substance and beasts
consent dwell

son hearkened gate of city
circumcised gate of city

came to pass
brothers took came killed

killed son took
out of house
went forth

sons came spoiled
defiled sister

took flocks herds asses
city field

wealth little ones wives took
spoiled house

troubled
made odious
inhabitants of land

gather together against
smite

destroyed

house

The Consolation of Poetry

I, too, have transitioned from oceanic bombast
to a barely updated revenue stream
chasing squirrels in the Chucky Cheese light
and criticising my eyes for allowing it
to numb my sense of Elf.

I've been there, gender-questioning man
lacrosse stick in hand, fibbing weaponry
like a clay soldier in a monastery gift shop.

In the florid haze of noon, knowing
everything disappears
into a frequency that's too good
for the heart to be prescribed.

In the artificial silence
you can hear the shared meter
of 'lock her up' and 'yes we can'
will only get you so far
beyond aplomb in this barbequed world.

I, too, have eaten Morning Star to evade
my all-seeing guilt, in a drive-thru
of the Mind, listening to cicada song
on loop in search of an encrypted sign
the world created for me.

The secret you hope to hear is the secret
you know: you are the future.
You will say things the world must evolve
to understand, then hate you for.
And it doesn't help to read about Joseph

or compare yourself to Esther.
The Enneagram is like a treasure map
to a lair that's been cemented with Reason.
Your horoscope is a column in Vogue.
You want to reach through two dimensions
and find a soul, and perhaps if you squint
the page will dance into particles.

So much ambiguity
is your clearest thought
and it's not even yours.
You're reading it on a subway ad
for a new dating app.

Because this is capitalism
your fantasy of being CEO
has come true. The company is yours.
And you are riding towards Yonkers
alone.

Mychal

*Then Mychal, daughter of Saul, looked out
and saw King David leaping and dancing before God
and she despised him.*

(2 Samuel 6:16)

The woman to my left says Mychal was jealous.
'She didn't want David exposing his junk.'

As if the very sheerness of it
might spill
into the womb-
vision of the onlookers.

The man next to her says it was more
of an image thing.
'The princess didn't want her father's lineage degraded
by displays of free abandon. A king should control himself.'

Does it matter whether the slave women saw
his underwear
or his manhood?

A bright nakedness or a formed shadow?'

Malbim says Mychal was too focused
on the outerwear.
This, from a man who never wore shorts.

A latecomer objects. The King never revealed a thing.
His 'accident' was carefully planned.
The impressive flesh in question was, in fact, a strap-on.

His husband counters
'While the flesh was David's own, it gave nothing away.
The onlookers couldn't learn anything
from studying his body
that wasn't already known on Instagram.'

We jostle nervously around the unexplained *Contempt*.
As if knowing David's crime could account for it.

Maybe the narrator wants us to believe
Mychal hated David *before* she looked
out the window, his dancing simply a trigger

or an excuse for something unspeakable
only wives can know.

Or perhaps the narrator needs us
to believe Mychal's jealousy
is for no one else but God.

David

They kissed one another,
and wept one with another,
until David exceeded.

(1 Samuel 20:41)

Saul hates himself for not being David.
And all David wants is to be loved by Saul.
Jonathan, the sage (or pushover) loves them both.

But Saul can only accept a love that excludes David
and since Jonathan can only love inclusively
he must exclude the excluder.

He hates Saul for making him hate him
and this is a sign of his great love.
And David?

Does he even love Jonathan?
No.
David is too concerned with Saul.

Why won't Saul realise the extra foreskins
were for *him*? That the nights David spent
practising the lyre were for *him*?

David wants the love of one who hates him.
Saul hates the one who most loves him.
And Jonathan loves two who do not care for him.

Psychologists say Saul is the superego,
David the id, and Jonathan the ego,
or some other combination.

Coaches say Saul is how we see ourselves,
Jonathan, how others see us,
and David how we would like to be seen.

The diagrams change with the business cycle
but never the text:
David, who never loved, wept the longest.

Two Great Lights

Two women came to Solomon's Court clutching an infant. One said, 'It's mine.' The other said, 'It's mine.' So Solomon adjudicated, 'Half is yours and half is yours.' But the real mother knew the truth wasn't worth splitting and sacrificed her child to the false mother. Better to live under illusion than be torn between realities. In that moment the wise King knew (according to the official version) she was the real mother.

In real life, however, the real mother was the false one. She knew the famous tale of Solomon and the two mothers and so was well prepared to convince the king of her intentions. Meanwhile, the real mother was a foreigner and was not privy to the lore of the land. Like the real mother in the official tale, she didn't want her child to be halved. But unlike her, she didn't understand the King's odd dialect. She thought it was mere idiom – meaning he would cast lots, or something only symbolically violent.

But some say, this, too, is only fable. The second woman wasn't a foreigner in the strict sense, but became one when she heard Solomon's order and remained silent.

These stories wouldn't matter except that each of us believes we are the child of that war between two mothers and of King Solomon's surrogate 'wisdom'.

And perhaps our belief is proof we really are.

Critics say the whole thing's an allegory. The two women correspond to Art and Religion. Art only wants the child if it's beautiful, whereas Religion wants it even if it's mutilated. Others say that 'God' was the first word for 'mine', and that Art gave it up when it saw that our life would be split in half.

Believing myself to be the child in question I am bound to disagree. I see my tale more as a retelling of an event that had nothing to do with us:

When God first created the sun and the moon, they were equal in size and radiance. But the moon asked, 'How can there be two great lights?' For it saw that complete equality contradicts Nature. So God told the moon to diminish itself. The moon knew this was unfair. 'Should I be punished just for asking an honest question?'

Nevertheless, it submitted.

Why?

Perhaps to preserve the phenomenon of light itself.

Thus, the real story is metaphysical. We are the lost light of a diminished moon, a light that has been subsumed and co-opted by the sun. Our true brightness is hidden by the concept of brightness which tricks our eyes into using the sun.

Lost and Found

People are fictions that have destinies, I wrote in 2014.
Lacking confidence, or else believing too much in the authority of
  the dead,
I attributed my words to imaginary rabbis.
Today, I am my own impresario.
I know it's easier to read about Sampson than to be him.
I know I am the sum of my miscalculated decisions
only if I say so.
The thoughts in my head may be someone else's lost property
in which case I have a duty to return them.
The Talmud teaches that if one finds multiple lost objects
one should return her own first, then her teacher's, and finally her
  parent's.
The thought that that thought belongs to my father is my teacher's
while the thought that that thought belongs to my teacher is my
  father's.
The result is that my cupboards are filled with commentaries
and my commentaries are filled with sock drawers.
I have spent my life between my father's house and my teacher's
discovering neither of them lives where they claim.
Because I have no billing address, I often catch the world looking
  for me.
In my world, I'm famous.
I'm on the Ten Most Wanted List for writers under the height of
  six feet.
I'm a moral example to those for whom my mediocre tennis skills
  show
I'm also human.
But enough about me. Where's the Lost and Found?

Opportunity Cost

The opportunity cost
of this line
hemmed by cowardice
and internalised stigma
is this one.
The opportunity
cost of speech
is breath.
The challenge of calling
breath an opportunity
is not lost
on this year's operations
manager. Go ask
the budget person
what a budget person means.
There's only so much
room for the appearance
of wisdom. The op-
in opportunity is different
than the op- in open
or opiates
is hardly helpful
at this time. Unfortunately
we aren't a great fit
for ourselves, though we en-
courage ourselves to try again
in the World to Come.
The opportunity to say
this opportunity only comes once
is your mantra
and is a performative contradiction
never arrives.
That is to say
its arrival is inopportune.
I am fortunate to say so, though

my portending leads me dangerously close
to pretension. Meanwhile, the
opalescence of a word like opulence
is a diversion from what's truly
figuratively on your heart. The opportunity
cost of pointing out what irony can't buy
is a deficit of self-exile,
leading to a deficit in justifications
of alienation.
You are on your own, whether you wear
khakis or a caftan; whether you spell
Hindu with a *u* deliberately or not.
The opportunity cost of growing up
in China is that your cat will not meow.
In Palestine, freedom will be the opposite
of occupation. One cannot name a place
without an opportunity cost. In America,
the cost is that you will think you are living
in America. The opportunity cost of gratitude
is demanding what you deserve.
What one wins on merit one loses on grace.
Jesus says we are entitled to nothing
but salvation. This allowed him to cash in
his asceticism for apotheosis. Good
for him. The opportunity cost of being
a Jew is seeing every standing structure
as a false god, a meager substitute
for a mythic Temple. Or else,
it is the fact that one must live with the secret
knowledge of one's inadequate truth.
Because I am a Jew, I cannot speak
to the opportunity cost of being
an antisemite, but I can marvel
at the irony that we invented self-hatred.
Or so we like to think,
since, being slaves, it is important for us
to prove our worth to the nations
who dwell within us.

Maybe only a slave would calculate opportunity cost.
So that's why we need Sabbath.
Or is Sabbath only the opportunity cost of work?
So that the cost of not keeping it is a world
where there is only opportunity cost?
'It's a good pitch,
but I don't think people would understand.'
'Don't sell them so short.'
I debate with myself until I am dying
and the opportunity cost of reflecting
is letting go.

Nineveh

An odd fact is that Jonah wanted to go to Nineveh.
It was on his bucket list.
He just didn't want to be a prophet.

As a student, he'd always dreamed
of visiting their fabled bakeries and libraries,
of observing the spectacular sacrifices to Baal.

In another life, he might even have fled *towards* Nineveh,
stuffed his ears with pitch and bitumen
and renounced the voices in his head.

But God had other plans,
and used Jonah,
making him doubly defiant,

a renunciate not only of divine commandment,
but of his own desire for a secular life.
As if it were the punch line to some dialectical joke

that can only be appreciated
by the depressive realists in heaven,
nothing could have been more pious

than boarding the ship to Tarsus.
It was by this sign that God knew Jonah
was prepared to convert the idolaters of the great city.

For the lesson of repentance that he needed
is that we must see our avoidance and our drive
as leading to the same place.

In the unedited version,
God shows Jonah that Nineveh was a Potemkin Village
made only for him:

The wicked foreigners
were copies of what he found distasteful in himself
and his own people.

An Israelite can never leave
his land, even if he calls it by a different name.
We children of Nineveh know this best:

No Torah, no 3,000-year history, no
prophecy or law can mute the voice
of heaven humming in our ears.

Elegy For A Special Kid

I

I remember the day Isaac came into my classroom,
out of breath with excitement.
'I can't do tomorrow's homework –
I'm going to Mount Moriah!'
He flashed his father's illegible note.
There were many things that made him a special kid.
His neck was shaped like a pill.
His head looked like an amulet.
His skin was translucent.

II

'If the story of Isaac teaches us anything
it's that every knife is a compliment
and the greatest sacrifice of all is to throw it away.'
My analyst reads from his new book, *Isaac*
at the release party.
'To disregard evidence of our worth
in favor of a faith that it does not depend on being chosen –
for death as for recognition –
is to become more and less than a hero –
is to become free.'

I wonder how being named *Isaac* led him
to become a self-described *healer*
and whether the positive coverage will help or hurt him.

III

I once read a Midrash
that Abraham offered Isaac the knife
and started to bind himself on the altar.
But the thought of killing his father was too much.
So Isaac removed the binding and placed himself in his stead.
This explains why there was no resistance. Why,
when Isaac got up, there were no bruises.
And why the ram seemed to die, of its own will
before the knife could fall.

Yom Kippur 2017

After Yehuda Amichai

On Yom Kippur, 2017, the year of DACA, I put on
my wedding *kittel* and walked through a city
that was neither old nor young.
For a long time, I stood in front of a poster
of the Old City of Jerusalem that was hanging
from a Chinatown bodega.
Outside Damascus Gate,
I could almost decipher a poet, dismounting
to confess a year's supply of regrets
to an Arab shopkeeper.
I lifted up my eyes to the corner
where a ram appeared, still and hornless,
afraid of its freedom.
The shop was full of shofars, dangling from the ceiling.
But deduction failed me.
Everything in sight was of antelope and oryx, blackbuck and addax.
Not a ram's horn to be found.
I searched until the light became so radiant I had to look away.
I couldn't stay to hear the poet's eloquence or its rebuttal.
I imagined ducks floating in the tears of both men,
swimming towards each other, hoping for a morsel of recognition.
When I finished, the time of the Closing of the Gates had passed.

Pirkei Avot

My father used to say:

Reader and writer are like two fugitives
Examining the shade of an egg.

But my mother would always counter, *an olive.*

Now, my children taunt me:

For what did they examine?
A place to rest? A secret measure?

The ward in which they question me
Becomes a palace I can almost see.

I strain towards the meager light
In search of something to say.

Look! The light is the size of an egg!
No, they reply. *An olive!*

Blackbirds

Blackbirds control our economy
is a dog whistle
said the rat whistlers
in the poem, in which, you said,
the symbolized is always superior
to the medium.

I said the dog whistlers are right
but that doesn't make it right
to agree (or disagree).

I was a blackbird passing
as a blackbird with no beak
and too much bark.

I was a whistle blower
ratting on language for selling us
the false hope truth would set us free.

It's not an exaggeration to say
correctness is a golden calf,
while righteousness is like a god
that tolerates no image.

I wanted to say, 'More than the blackbirds have observed anti-
    blackbirdism
anti-blackbirdism has observed the blackbirds,'
but knew better.

You can take a blackbird out of [   ]
but you can't take the [   ] out of

I'd be lying to myself if I said my skepticism went all the way down.

First they came for the bizarro billionaires

and I spoke up.
Then they came for the fake twitter accounts and again I spoke up.
Then they came for the opioid epidemic
and I spoke up.
But when they came for me, my trial period had expired.
Don't worry, said customer service.
An upgrade is just the cost of a malaria net.
So I upgraded.
And that is why I am now speaking up
for only $5.99/month.

In every generation, they have stood against us,
but we blackbirds have prevailed.
And they have the gall to call our prevalence a conspiracy!

We were anti-blackbird ourselves, before there was such a thing as
    anti-blackbirdism.
That is why we are so proud
and demand that anyone who accuses us of wanting to endure is an
    anti-blackbird,
since they force us to lose our focus on God and focus on anti-
    blackbirdism.
On the other hand, nobody can make you lose focus on God
    without your permission.

Take comfort in the Lord, O ye blackbirds of little faith.
For I have told you, O blackbird, what is good and what the
    language requires:
Love love, act actionably, and fly humbly with your projections.
The rest is commentary. Go and earn it.

Why You No Longer Pray Amongst the Ruins

You used to think the prophet was there
to protect you
from the sound of God's infinite sadness –

You would run past every DO NOT ENTER
to hear the hidden echo of your heart
cooing like a misplaced dove.

You preferred the risk of bandits
and wild beasts to the certainty
of foreshortened prayer.

In those days, you were never afraid
of suspicion or collapse
or demons.

Now that you have heard the voiceling
you understand what the prophet meant
and have become him.

You no longer wander off the path
to find yourself in piles of debris.
You understand the boundaries

that they are there not for you,
but the Master of the Universe,
lest the Holy One die of a broken heart.

Doorknob Poem

Our time is up.
But wait, I haven't gotten to my volta!
You can make one last point.
My point is that phenomenology takes for granted that we are
always arriving at things from somewhere.
'To the things themselves' presupposes the very natural attitude
we are asked to 'suspend.' No natural attitude, no epoché.
But that's also not my point. If it were, I wouldn't be writing this as a
  poem.
My point is that just as revelation is an exodus, so is what we call thinking.
But, that's also not accurate.
I'm sorry but I have another client. I'm afraid I'm going to have to ask
  you to leave.
I'm confused. Are you going to ask me, or did you just ask me?
And why are you afraid?
I did ask. Security!

Without Without Title

A poem that admits there is no meaning
besides the gathering of syllables
into little bouquets of desire,
placed, somewhere, between light and dust,
is said to need, as winter needs,
the beauty of visible breath. If
wisdom is not to be had, it is to be sung.
A poem is nothing but the sound of emptiness
enfleshed, or else the sound
of a half-naked emptiness
caught between an urge to strip,
a want to decorate,
and a lingering contentment
to stay here

Acknowledgements

Divine guidance is a mystery. I thank my beloved A.W., muse, co-author, and brilliant reader of this work and our shared life. I dedicate *Nineveh* to you. Thank you to my parents and grandparents for raising me to love art and literature, my brother and sister, for being my first instructors in perspectivalism, and my dear teachers who modeled humility and awe despite their expertise. Thank you, Helen Kuryllo and Joseph Pucci, for opening my heart to poetry in my formative years. Thank you, Mychal Springer, for teaching me the meditation exercise known as 'theological reflection', which provided the seeds for some of my Midrashic poems. Thank you, Stephen Ross, *akhi*, for your incisive edits on early drafts of *Nineveh*, for your luminous reading suggestions, and for our epically generative correspondence in which a number of the poems in this book first took form. Thank you, Aaron Belz, for making me laugh, and inspiring my work with your weird, profound humor. Thank you, Ari Resnikoff, for being my bridge to Yiddish modernism and exemplifying an uncompromisingly experimental voice. Thank you, Willy Oppenheim, for teaching me to hold the hand of emptiness. Thank you, Ian Pindar, for awarding me the *Oxonian Prize* and encouraging me at the earliest stages of this work.

Thank you to my generous and deeply spirited editor, Michael Schmidt, for championing my work and helping it become a better version of itself. Thank you Jazmine Linklater, Andrew Latimer, Luke Allan and the Carcanet team for helping bringing this work to light.

Thank you to the editors of the publications in which my poems first appeared: *Blackbox Manifold, Eborakon, Four Way Review, Glasgow Review of Books, Haaretz, Lehrhaus, Mantis, Molly Bloom, New Poetries VII, PN Review, Supplement, Tenebrae, TYPO, The Oxonian Review*, and *Wave Composition*.